Tidy Up!

Gwenyth Swain

First Avenue Editions/Minneapolis

small world

To find out more about the pictures in this book, turn to page 22.
To find out more about sharing this book with children, turn to page 24.

The photographs in this book are used with the permission of: © Linda Phillips/Photo Researchers, Inc., front cover; © Paul A. Souders/CORBIS, back cover; © Trip/M. Fairman, p. 1; © Trip/A. Semashko, p. 3; © Liba Taylor/CORBIS, p. 4; © Richard Hutchings/Photo Researchers, Inc., p. 5; © Bill Bachman, p. 6; © Bachman/Photo Researchers, Inc., p. 7; © Peter Turnley/CORBIS, p. 8; © Trip/H. Rogers, p. 9; © Trip/P. Mercea, p. 10; © Mark E. Gibson/Visuals Unlimited, Inc., p. 11; © Laura Dwight/CORBIS, pp. 12, 21; © M. Bryan Ginsberg, pp. 13, 14, 18; © Jeff Greenberg/Visuals Unlimited, Inc., p. 15; © Trip/J. Sweeney, p. 16; © Kevin R. Morris/CORBIS, p. 17; © Ecoscene/CORBIS, p. 19; © K. Cavanagh/Photo Researchers, Inc., p. 20.

First Avenue Editions
An imprint of Lerner Publishing Group
241 First Avenue North
Minneapolis, MN 55401 U.S.A.

Website address: www.lernerbooks.com

Library of Congress Cataloging-in-Publication Data

Swain, Gwenyth, 1961–
    Tidy up! / by Gwenyth Swain.
        p.   cm. — (Small world)
    Includes index.
    ISBN: 1-57505-160-5 (pbk. : alk. paper)
    1. House cleaning—Juvenile literature. 2. Orderliness—Juvenile literature. I. Title. II. Small world (Minneapolis, Minn.)
    TX324 .S93 2002
    648'.5—dc21   2001003597

Manufactured in the United States of America
1 2 3 4 5 6 - JR - 07 06 05 04 03 02

What do you do to make things tidy?

Do you clean up after yourself?

Do you pitch in when others need help?

There are big messes, small messes,
and messes in between.

And every single one of them needs
to be cleaned.

So fill a tub.

Soap, rinse, and scrub.

Beat it or sweep it.

Shake it or rake it.

Fold your clothes.
Stack them in a pile.

Make things neat.
You'll make others smile.

Do you need to do chores before
you can play?

Then shoo, shoo dust bunnies!
Get out of the way!

Messes look like mountains until
someone lends a hand.

So grab yourself a broom.
Help clean the grounds.

Straighten up.

Share the load.

Scrub it clean together.

Tidy up as you go!

More about the Pictures

Front cover: Asian American siblings tidy up their room.

Back cover: A girl sweeps the courtyard of her school on Panay, an island in the Philippines.

Page 1: A young English girl helps wash up in the kitchen.

Page 3: A boy in Moscow, Russia, takes out the trash.

Page 4: Everyone helps clean up after a meal in Kigoma Refugee Camp in Tanzania.

Page 5: In the United States, three kids work together to bathe their dog.

Page 6: A group of Australian schoolchildren clean up roadside litter near the town of Thallon.

Page 7: This American third grader has a lot to clean up when he's done with his art project.

Page 8: A girl in Chiapas, Mexico, helps her mother do the laundry by filling a tub.

Page 9: People work hard scrubbing tiles at a temple in India.

Page 10: In Cozia, Romania, a boy carries a bundle of brooms for sweeping up messes.

Page 11: Children in California work together to rake fall leaves.

Page 12: Piles of clean laundry grow higher and higher as this boy helps his father in New York City.

Page 13: A boy in Guatemala tidies up by folding a blanket neatly.

Page 14: In Sri Lanka, a girl gathers water for clean-up time.

Page 15: Vacuuming is an important chore for this American boy in New Jersey.

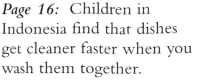

Page 16: Children in Indonesia find that dishes get cleaner faster when you wash them together.

Page 17: In Thailand a group of boys makes a clean sweep of the temple grounds.

Page 18: A boy in Mexico helps clean up.

Page 19: In England children share the job of recycling by putting their drink cans in the proper bin.

Page 20: A father and son soap and scrub their car.

Page 21: This eleven-year-old girl tidies up by ironing her own clothes.

A Note to Adults on Sharing This Book

Help your child become a lifelong reader. Read this book together, taking turns as you both read out loud. Look over the photographs and choose your favorites. Sound out new words and go back to them later for review. Then try these "extensions"—activities that extend the experience of reading and build discussion and problem-solving skills.

Talk about Cleaning
All around the world, people young and old work hard to keep things neat and tidy. Have your child describe the things he or she does to tidy up around the house, at school, or in the community. Next, study this book together. Which activities does your child do? Ask your child which clean-up chores he or she does every day, once a week, or never. If your child says never, ask if he or she wants to try doing the chore, either now or in the future.

Tidy Up Together
With your child, talk about the different things you do to tidy up. Choose one chore that you can do together at least once a week. Could your child lend you a hand in cleaning the car or in washing the dishes? Discuss new ways you could tidy up together. How about taking a trash bag along the next time you and your child go for a walk, picking up trash as you go? Or how about offering to help a neighbor weed the garden, rake leaves, or shovel snow?